How Should I Dress?

Ashley S. Burell

Rigby.
A Harcourt Achieve Imprint

www.Rigby.com
1-800-531-5015

You can play outside
in many kinds of weather.

On rainy days,
you can play
in puddles.

On snowy days,
you can build
snowmen.

3

When the weather changes, make sure you change your clothes, too!

On sunny days, wear clothes to keep you cool.

On windy days, wear clothes to keep you warm.

It's rainy, it's rainy.
How should you dress?
What should you wear?
What is your guess?

sandals   shorts   raincoat

A raincoat is a great choice
for a rainy day.
Rain boots and hats
will also help keep you dry.

It's snowy, it's snowy.
How should you dress?
What should you wear?
What is your guess?

hat   shorts   swimsuit

A hat will keep your head
warm on a snowy day.
Mittens and a coat are also
great for sledding in the snow.

It's sunny, it's sunny.
How should you dress?
What should you wear?
What is your guess?

mittens   shorts   scarf

Shorts are great
for a sunny day.
When you play
with your pail at the beach,
you might wear a swimsuit.

It's windy, it's windy.
How should you dress?
What should you wear?
What is your guess?

sandals   jacket   swimsuit

A jacket is a good choice
for a windy day.
Sweaters and hats
will also keep you warm
when you fly a kite.

It's stormy, it's stormy.
How should you dress?
What should you wear?
What is your guess?

Wait a minute,
there's a storm today.
You should stay inside
to play!

weather	clothes
rainy	
snowy	
sunny	
windy	